TEACHING MIDDLE GRADERS TO USE PROCESS WRITING SKILLS

Strategies, Techniques, and Activities

by Marilyn Seguin

Incentive Publications, Inc.
Nashville, Tennessee

For Katy, who likes to write

Cover and Illustrations by Geoffrey Brittingham
Edited by Leslie Britt

ISBN 0-86530-299-5

PRINTED IN THE UNITED STATES OF AMERICA

Table of Contents

Part IV—Writing Projects **53-79**

INTRODUCTION

Dear Teacher:

Learning how to write involves a lot of hard work. Many students would rather do just about anything other than tackle a writing project. This resource guide can change your students' attitudes about writing. The writing techniques and projects suggested on these pages can make an "I hate to write" student say, "Hey, writing is kind of fun!"

- Part I introduces four creative prewriting ideas. These techniques are designed to help students *think* about how and what they will write before they begin the endeavor.

- Part II presents techniques for the writing process: ways to get creative ideas out of the students' heads and onto their papers.

- Part III offers innovative approaches to evaluating finished pieces of writing. These revision techniques help students to identify strengths and weaknesses in their own and others' writing.

- Part IV offers ideas for stimulating and challenging writing projects. Students can apply the techniques learned in Parts I, II, and III to help them tackle these projects or any other writing assignments they may encounter. Every activity description includes teacher directions, a list of materials needed, a time frame for completion of the project, and, when applicable, reproducibles.

Teaching Middle Graders To Use Process Writing Skills can permanently change the way your students approach a writing assignment. Once they have tried the ideas in this book, your students will find writing to be an exciting and rewarding experience.

PART I

Prewriting Techniques

Where to begin? Getting started can be a young writer's most difficult task. The process of writing begins with **thinking** about writing. The activities presented in Part I are designed to give students an opportunity to think about writing and to make planning decisions before they begin the first draft of a writing assignment.

Warm Up

To the Teacher:

In sports, athletes do warm-up exercises to get going. Writers can benefit by warming up as well. The following activity is aimed at getting your students limbered up by writing fun stuff first. Your students will then be ready to tackle any writing assignment you give them. The idea is to think and talk first, then to write. Students may write one sentence or a page. Tell them that whatever they write during the warm-up stage will not be graded.

Materials:

A "grab bag" filled with small household objects: an earring, a pencil, a paper clip, a piece of candy, a light bulb, a sock, etc.

Time Frame:

Introduction and explanation of activity — 10 minutes
Group discussions — 10 minutes
Individual writing time — 10 minutes

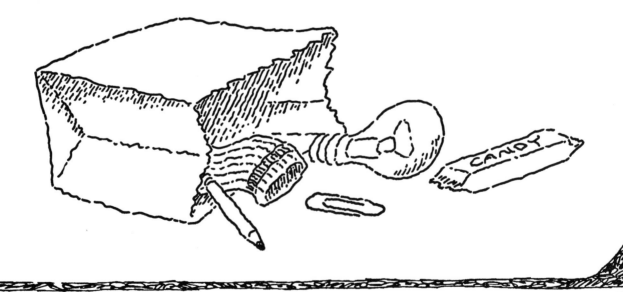

Warm-Up Activity

1. Divide the class into small groups of 4 or 5 students. Allow one student from each group to pull one object from the "grab bag."

2. Explain to everyone that this is an "I" exercise. For the next ten minutes, students should discuss within their groups what it would be like to be the object drawn from the "grab bag." In other words, the students should get "inside" the object and give it a life.

3. When the ten-minute discussion is over, tell students to take out paper and pencil and write from the perspective of the object about which they have been talking.

Other Warm-Up Activities

- Ask students to open a book—any book. Tell each student to close his or her eyes and put a finger on the page. Tell them to open their eyes and write about the word pointed to—anything that comes to mind—for five minutes.

- Read the first line of a book from the library. Ask students to think of and write a second line; ask them to write the last line for the story.

- Tell students to write a note to the person sitting next to them, telling that person what kind of day it's been.

- Collect interesting pictures and glue them to cardboard. Let students choose a picture on which to base a warm-up exercise.

Journaling

To the Teacher:

Youngsters can improve their writing skills in a number of ways by keeping a daily journal. A journal gives students daily practice in writing. It also provides a rich resource of thoughts, observations, and responses that can be developed by students into full-fledged essays or stories. Most young students will equate "journal" with "diary." When asked to keep a journal, these students may simply record the date, the weather, and what the school cafeteria served at lunch. You can help students "structure" their journals so that they can draw from their journal entries when they need ideas for stories, essays, or poetry. Two structures for journaling are given on the following pages. Choose one or alternate them as you encourage students to keep a daily journal.

Materials:

Reproducibles for one or both of the journal activities (pages 15 and 18)

Time Frame:

Allow ten minutes each day for journal-writing time. Encourage students to make journal entries for weekends and holidays as well.

Journaling Activity #1

The Dialogue Journal

1. Pass out dialogue journal pages (reproducible form, page 15) to students. Discuss the meaning of dialogue (engaging one another in conversation) and ask students to share examples of two-way conversations they have had during that day.

2. Explain to students that they will be given time each day to record a dialogue that has taken place in the past twenty-four hours. Remind them that dialogues need not take place between two people. For example, a dialogue may take place between you and your pet cat; between you and your stomach; or between the serious side of you and the fun side of you.

3. Encourage your students to use their journals when they write stories, essays, and poems.

My Dialogue Journal

Recently I had a talk with (who or what) _my goldfish_

We talked a lot about (what) _whether or not he worries about things._

This dialogue occurred at (where) _home in my bedroom_

on (when) _January 12th_

It all began when I said: _I don't want to give this book report. I hate giving book reports. It makes me so nervous and I can't eat beforehand. I worry about what everyone is thinking about how I look and what I say. I don't even like this book! I'll bet it's nice to be a goldfish and swim around and eat._

Voice 2 (The Response): _Yeah, sure, but I don't have friends. I never get to go out. I can't laugh and have fun either. It's boring being a fish_

My Dialogue Journal

Recently I had a talk with (who or what) _____.

We talked a lot about (what) _____.

This dialogue occurred at (where) _____

on (when) _____.

It all began when I said:

Voice 2 (The Response):

Journaling Activity #2

The Sensory Journal

1. Pass out sensory journal pages to students (repro-
    ducible form, page 18). Prepare a poster that lists a
    variety of sensory experiences: chocolate ice-cream
    cone, my locker, pizza, Thanksgiving, a visit to the
    dentist, our school cafeteria, the playground after it
    rains, apples, my favorite flower, old books, getting up
    in the morning, falling asleep at night, a hot bath, etc.
    Post the list of sensory experiences where all the
    students can see it.

2. Together, fill out a sample page for the object "chocolate
    ice-cream cone." Encourage the students to include as
    much detail as possible in the description, especially for
    the not-so-obvious category of "hearing." What sounds
    do we associate with eating ice cream? The sound of the
    lever on the utensil that releases the scoop of ice cream
    onto the cone? The crunch of the cone as we bite into
    it? Tell students that it is all right to leave blanks if they
    can't think of any associations.

3. Tell students that they will be given time each day to record an entry in their sensory journals. They may write about an object they have experienced or one from the list.

4. Encourage students to use their journal entries when they write stories, essays, and poems.

My Sensory Journal

Today, I want to describe _____

_____

Sight Memory:

Sound Memory:

Taste Memory:

Smell Memory:

Touch Memory:

Talk It Out On Tape

To the Teacher:

Most of us are more comfortable speaking our thoughts than writing them. What we say is almost always more clear than what we write. Some students find it helpful to "talk out" their ideas to someone else before they put their words on paper. Some of my students find it helpful to tape-record their thoughts for a writing assignment. They can then listen to and transcribe their ideas. Try out the tape recorder technique in your own classroom using the activity below, or with your own writing assignment topic.

Materials:

- Cassette tape recorders
- Blank cassette tapes
  (Tip: Get cassettes that are screwed together rather than glued. If the tape jams from frequent rewinds, you can unscrew the cassette case and fix the tape.)
- A set of comic strip cards for each group
  (Cut simple newspaper comic strips such as B.C., Peanuts, or Cathy, and paste onto cardboard. Cut apart each cartoon frame and secure with a rubber band—one comic strip sequence per set.)

Time Frame:

- Think time—5 minutes
- Tape time—15 minutes per group

19

Talk It Out Activity

1. Divide class into groups of 3 or 4. Distribute a tape recorder and blank cassette tape to each group. Give each group one set of comic strip cards.

2. Ask each group to arrange the cartoon cards into a sequence that will best illustrate a story.

3. After each group decides on the best arrangement for the cartoon cards, instruct them to talk out the story into the tape recorder.

   Only two rules apply:
   > Each student in the group must participate in recording the story.

   > The recorded story must not backtrack or repeat itself. (It may take several tries before each group is satisfied with its recording.)

Brainstorm!

To the Teacher:

Brainstorming is a group activity practiced quite often in the business world. This technique allows the ideas presented by one person to stimulate ideas in others. In the classroom, brainstorming can help students find fresh approaches to writing even if everyone is instructed to write on the same topic. Brainstorming can help students overcome the uncomfortable feeling of not knowing how to begin when they sit down to write.

Materials:

- Chalkboard or flip chart on which to list students' ideas
- Poster of brainstorming rules:

RULES FOR BRAINSTORMING

1. When a student has an idea to share, he or she should raise his or her hand to be recognized.

2. Everyone should contribute at least one idea.

3. Establish a nonjudgmental atmosphere—no idea should be ridiculed or discarded. Everyone should be encouraged to speak whatever ideas come to mind.

Time Frame:

- Brainstorming session—20 minutes
- Individual evaluation of idea list—10 minutes

Brainstorming Activity

1. Assign a topic on which you want your students to write a poem, essay, or story. Use your own topic or try one of the following: my family, a lucky day, money, how I feel about year-round schooling, the book we just read, getting along with my family. Write the topic on the board or a flip chart.

2. Post the brainstorming rules poster and discuss with the class.

3. Begin the brainstorming session by asking students to raise their hands when they have an idea about the topic. Record every idea, no matter how silly it may seem!

4. At the end of the twenty-minute session, ask students to copy the brainstorming list into their own notebooks. Tell them to go through the list and cross out ideas that don't interest them or that they think won't work. Don't discuss individual lists—students should feel free to evaluate the ideas on their own.

5. Tell students to pick one of the remaining ideas on which to base a writing assignment—each individual should choose an idea about which he or she can see him- or herself writing. This idea will be the focus of the writing assignment for that student. (For example, the topic "my family" might yield a brainstorming list that includes parents and siblings, grandparents, cousins, everyone different, look-alike. One student might focus on writing a family essay about his grandparents; another might focus the assignment on how the members of her family look alike while they are very different in personality.)

Writing Techniques

Some people call the writing stage "drafting." The first or "rough draft" of any piece of writing requires the student to get ideas out of his or her head and onto paper. The techniques for writing presented in Part II aim to enable students to make rough drafts of their writing assignments.

You can use these Writing Techniques with the activities described in this book or with your own writing assignments. See Part IV for a list of writing assignment ideas that use techniques from all three stages of the writing process—prewriting, writing, and revision. By building on the ideas in this book, you can help your students have fun when they write!

Freewriting in the Dark

To the Teacher:

Freewriting is an activity in which a writer starts with a topic and writes nonstop anything that comes to mind on the subject. Freewriting is an excellent way to create a rough draft. It is most effective when done in the dark. Without light, the writer is forced to keep writing, rather than tempted to correct and revise. The student can later read over the freewritten draft and then formulate an outline on which to base revisions.

Materials:

A timer

Time Frame:

5 minutes

Freewriting Activity

1. Begin with a specific topic. Tell students to write the name of the topic at the tops of their papers.

2. Tell the students that you want them to write whatever comes to mind concerning the topic. Remind them that this is only a rough draft, and they should not worry about spelling and punctuation. Explain that for this reason you're going to turn off the lights so that they can't see what they've written until the time is up. The rules: Write quickly and don't stop until the time is up. Set the timer for five minutes and let them begin.

3. When the freewriting time is up, turn on the lights and let the students read over what they have written. They can now begin to develop an outline from the freewriting.

The Reporter's Way

To the Teacher:

News reporters employ a formula for asking questions at interviews. This formula is called the 5 W's—who, what, where, when, and why. Getting answers to these five questions ensures that the reporter will have most of what he or she needs to write a story. Students can use these same five questions as probes to their own ideas for a specific writing topic. Answers to the 5 W's create a decent first draft for many classroom writing assignments, especially reports.

Materials:

Reproducible copies of the 5 W's (page 29)

Time Frame:

No limit

Activity

1. Distribute copies of the 5 W's reproducible and instruct students to fill in the topic line.

2. Ask students to think about the topic with regard to each of the W's. Students should write at least one paragraph for each W. They may answer each W based on what they already know about the topic, or you may instruct them to do outside interviews or book research.

3. Discuss ideas with the class. Decide which of the W's are most important for the topic, and which W's might be eliminated. Tell students to arrange their ideas into an outline for the assignment.

The Reporter's Notebook

Assignment_____

Directions: You are a reporter. Your editor has assigned you to cover the topic listed at the top of this page. Ask the following questions about your topic:

Who?

What?

When?

Where?

Why?

Storyboarding

To the Teacher:

The storyboarding technique was invented by Walt Disney, who used it to plan animated and live-action film sequences. Walt wanted to see the complete story line displayed before him as he and his staff planned every twist of the plot. The storyboard is also a useful tool for student writers. It allows them to arrange pieces of information as they write. Students revise as they write by physically moving pieces of information around, even adding or discarding ideas as needed.

Materials:

- 5' by 7' sheet of cork board
- Straight pins or tacks
- 2" squares of paper
- 28 3" x 5" index cards

(Note: Students may take turns using the cork board equipment, or the teacher can act as facilitator while the class plans out the story as a group. For individual storyboard planning, I ask my students to use small adhesive notes to record their ideas. These notes can be stuck and unstuck repeatedly without damage to desk top or wall.)

Time Frame:

30–60 minutes for each activity

Storyboarding Activity #1

1. To demonstrate the storyboarding technique, assign the topic: "What we did in school yesterday." Across the top of the board, pin squares of paper labeled 8 A.M., 9 A.M., 10 A.M., and so on. Ask students to talk about what they did at each time. Write their ideas on 2″ square note papers and pin these in a vertical row under the appropriate time label.

2. When all the ideas are pinned, ask students to write a brief essay based on the storyboard.

3. Clean off the storyboard, stacking the idea squares. Pin up three new labels across the top of the storyboard—Work, Play, Other. Read through the stack of idea squares and pin them in vertical rows underneath whichever label the students say is most appropriate. (What do the ideas pinned under "other" have in common?)

4. When the stack is exhausted, ask students to write a brief essay based on the new storyboard.

5. Discuss the essays, using the following questions as guides:

   • Which storyboard was easier to write from?

   • Which essay is more interesting?

   • What other labels might we have used to organize a storyboard about the topic "What we did in school yesterday"?

Storyboarding Activity #2

1. Prepare four storyboard labels as follows:

   Card #1: Me

   Card #2: My Companion

   Card #3: Setting

   Card #4: The Problem

Tack the four label cards across the top of the cork board.

2. Divide the remaining cards into four piles (Me, My Companion, Setting, The Problem). Label as follows:

ME CARDS	MY COMPANION CARDS	SETTING CARDS
astronaut	a magician	the beach
professional athlete	pet dog	the desert
Super Kid	the President	a dark cave
spy	brother or sister	the zoo
inventor	best friend	a cruise ship
reporter	worst enemy	amusement park

THE PROBLEM CARDS

You're stuck in the past, and you want to return to the present.

The game is tied, and it's up to you to lead your team to victory.

You meet an alien who is stranded on earth.

You have to get away from a troublesome ghost.

You are trying to locate buried treasure.

You must restore the Queen's lost jewels.

3. Ask a student to choose one card from each of the four piles and pin them to the storyboard underneath the corresponding label cards.

4. Inform the class that they now have the four elements of a story idea. Beginning with the Me category, ask for suggestions about the main character (for example, "What he is wearing? What does she look like?"). Have a student write down the suggestions on 2″ squares of paper and pin them under the Me card. Proceed with the My Companion, Setting, and Problem categories.

5. When the storyboard is filled and ideas are exhausted, ask students to copy the storyboard ideas into their notebooks. They will use these ideas to create an outline for a story.

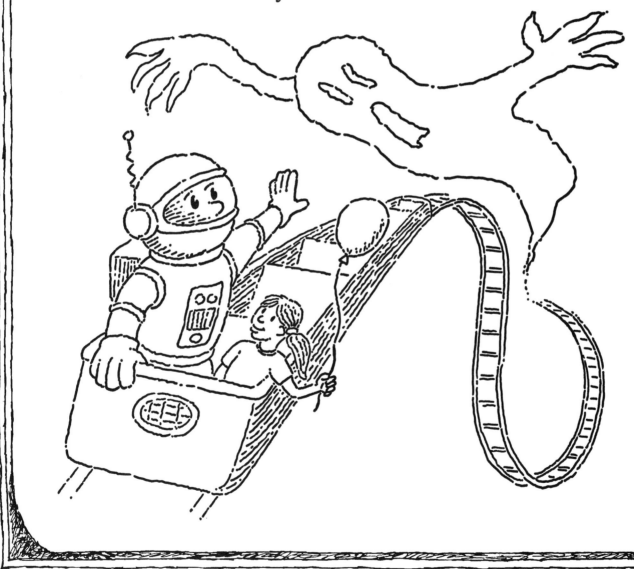

Satellite Outlines

To the Teacher:

The satellite outline technique is a variation of a method called "clustering," developed by Gabrielle Rico and explained in her book *Writing the Natural Way*. According to Rico, clustering allows writers to record their creative thoughts in a clear and logical way. Later they can use the cluster, or satellite outline, as a plan for a finished piece of writing. Below you will find an example of a satellite outline for the activity on page 35.

Materials:

Unlined paper

Time Frame:

15–20 minutes

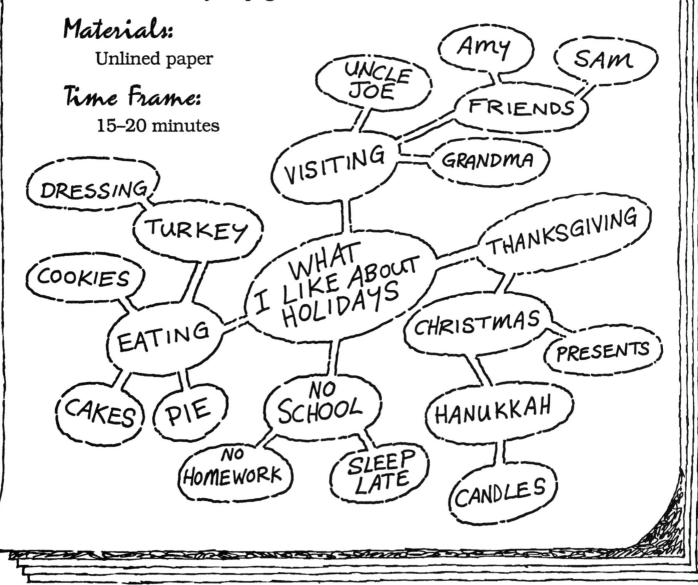

Satellite Outline Activity

1. Pass out unlined paper. Tell students to write in the center of the page the idea about which you want them to write. For this activity, the idea will be "Things I like about holidays."

2. Tell students to draw a circle around the topic and to think about it.

3. Tell students to write an idea about the topic anywhere on the page, to circle that idea, and to draw a line from it to the topic. Now students will have two circled ideas on the page.

4. Instruct students to write another idea inspired by either circle, to circle the third idea, and to draw a line from it to the idea which inspired it. Continue in this way until the page is filled or students run out of ideas. (You might show students the sample outline on the previous page, then put it away and let them create their own.)

5. Now it's time to organize the ideas for writing. Tell students to look over their satellite outlines and select the most important idea associated with "What I like most about holidays." They should mark that idea circle with a star. Ask students to use the satellite to write an essay, beginning with the idea they have starred.

PART III

Revision Techniques

Anyone who writes regularly knows that revision is the real work of writing. Young writers often need revision strategies to help them "see" their writing as something more than just words on a page. The following challenging revision strategies are aimed toward helping your students see their writing in a new way so that they can revise and improve their work.

GLUE

Cut and Paste

To the Teacher:

If your students use computers in the classroom, they may already know how to revise their writing by moving words, sentences, and paragraphs around on the computer screen. Students and teachers, however, don't always have access to computers when they write. The good news is that they don't need advanced technology to reorganize their work. Students can use scissors and glue sticks to reorganize their rough drafts: first, they cut apart elements (words, sentences, paragraphs) of their rough drafts; then they arrange those elements into a revised second draft, pasting down the elements to a clean sheet of paper. They then write a third (and usually final) draft of their work from this paste-up sheet. Use the following activity to introduce this cut-and-paste revision technique to your students. Then have them try it on their own rough drafts.

Materials:

- Glue sticks or paste
- Unlined paper
- Copies of the reproducible story on pages 40–41
- Scissors

Time Frame:

20 minutes

Cut and Paste Activity

1. Reproduce the story on pages 40 and 41 to provide one for each student. Cut the paragraphs apart on the dotted lines and place each cut-up story in an envelope. Students may work in groups for this activity.

2. Distribute glue sticks or paste and unlined paper to students. Distribute envelopes with cut-up stories.

3. Explain that each envelope contains an entire story. Ask students to arrange the pieces into a revised draft. Tell them to look for transitions or word signals at the beginning of each piece as clues to the sequence of the story. When students have arranged the pieces, tell them to glue them to the sheet of unlined paper.

4. Discuss the student revisions. You might want to project a transparency of the original story onto the wall so that students can see what it looked like before you cut it. Show how the word signals at the beginnings of the paragraphs give clues to the sequence of the story.

5. Tell students to use the scissors to cut and paste new revisions as the discussion continues.

Do What You Can
(An Indian Legend)

A long time ago, an Indian princess tended a large field
of corn outside her village. She carefully hoed and weeded
between the rows of corn, but no matter how hard she
worked, she saw that the corn was withering from lack of
rain. As she hoed, she looked up at the sky, hoping for rain.

But each day was as dry as the day before.

One day, the princess stood in her field looking up at the
sky in despair. Two raindrops looked down and saw her.
One raindrop said to the other:

"I feel sorry for the princess. She has taken such good
care of the corn, but it does not grow for lack of rain."

"Yes," said the other raindrop, "but you are only one
tiny raindrop. What can you do? You cannot water the
whole field."

"Well," said the first raindrop, "I cannot water the whole field, that is true. But I can cheer up the princess. I'll go to the field to show the princess that I want to help her. Here I go."

"Well, if you are going, I'll come too," said the other raindrop.

The raindrops fell to earth. The first one fell right on the princess's nose and the other fell on a stalk of corn.

"Oh my," said the princess, smiling. "I felt a raindrop. Perhaps we'll have a shower and my corn will be saved!" And she began to laugh and sing.

Up in the sky, a great many raindrops heard the princess laughing and singing in her cornfield. The raindrops gathered together to see what was happening. When they saw that their companions had fallen to earth to cheer the princess and water the corn, one said:

"Our two companions have done much good down below. Let's join them on their good errand." And down fell the raindrop. "Me, too," said another, and another, and another. Soon, a whole shower had fallen to earth and the cornfield was watered.

The corn grew and ripened—all because the first tiny raindrop had been determined to do what it could.

Peer Editing

To the Teacher:

Students can help one another revise their writing. Ultimately it is the reader, not the writer, who must determine whether a piece of writing is clear and interesting. If time permits, peer editing should take place every time a writing assignment is completed and before the assignment is turned in to the teacher. Allow students plenty of time to make revisions and corrections based on their peers' suggestions. The following peer editing activity sets forth guidelines for this revision technique.

Materials:

Copies of the reproducible on page 44

Time Frame:

15 or 20 minutes, based on length of the writing assignment being edited

Peer Editing Checklist

Editor's name _Jessica Zellars_

Date _January 28_

Writer's name _David Hirshbrunner_

Title of work _Summer Vacation_

Read

Overall, is the writing clear? _Yes, but needs more explanation of summer plans_

Overall, is the writing interesting?

Peer Editing Activity

1. On the day that a draft of a writing assignment is due, ask students to pair off and exchange drafts. Distribute one copy of the reproducible checklist to each student.

2. Explain peer editing. Tell students that good editors follow three steps when they examine a writer's work. Write the three steps on the board:
   A. Read silently.
   B. Examine closely.
   C. Listen to what the writer tells you about the work.

3. Ask students to follow these three steps as they look over the work of their peers. Tell students to write their comments on the checklist.

4. After 15 or 20 minutes, ask students to discuss their peer editing checklists with their partners. Based on the discussion, they should decide whether or not to make additional revisions to their work.
   (Note: Peer editing is a noisy activity. Students become excited and enthusiastic as they discuss their work with one another. That's what makes this technique fun.)

5. You may wish to have students turn in their peer editing sheets with their assignments so that you can assess how significant the peer suggestions were to the revision process.

Peer Editing Checklist

Editor's name _____

Date _____

Writer's name _____

Title of work _____

Read

    Overall, is the writing clear?

    Overall, is the writing interesting?

Examine

    Does the beginning capture your attention or interest?

    Are there clues (transitions) as to what to expect as you read along?

    Does the ending give the reader a sense of conclusion?

    Is the writing grammatically correct?

    Are all words spelled correctly?

Listen

    (To the editor: Ask the writer the following questions and record his or her responses.)

    What did you learn from writing this piece?

    What do you like most about this piece?

    What do you like least?

    How do you plan to revise this draft?

Proofread Out Loud

To the Teacher:

Young writers don't need to understand the concepts of grammar in order to improve their writing. Few writers realize that their ears are just as reliable as their eyes in revising written work. Give your students enough time to proofread their work out loud to one another so that they can listen to the way it sounds. Many times, when a student hears what has been written, he or she is led to make changes that vastly improve the work. At the very least, the technique of proofreading out loud will help your students find and eliminate their grammatical errors. A recent study at City University of New York showed that proofreading aloud automatically eliminated sixty percent of students' grammatical errors. Proofreading out loud can even help students spot spelling errors more quickly. Encourage students to keep a dictionary handy when they proofread their work, and to look up any word of which they are uncertain. The following activity is designed to show students how to proofread for spelling errors.

Materials:

- Copies of the reproducible story on page 48
- Unlined index cards
- Dictionaries

Time Frame:

20 minutes

Proofreading Activity

1. Distribute copies of the reproducible story on page 48. Ask students to read the story silently and to circle words they think might be spelled incorrectly.

2. When they are finished, ask them to count the number of words they circled as incorrect spellings. Inform them that there are 18 misspelled words in the story—most students will be surprised that there are so many.

3. Distribute index cards to each student. Instruct the students to place the index cards over the story so that only the bottom line of words is showing. Beginning with the last word of the story, students should begin to quietly read aloud from the story backwards, uncovering one word at a time.

4. Take the students through the words of the last line, one by one. Does the word "heard" look as though it is spelled correctly? Continue on with "ever," "I," "excuse," and so on. If a student tells you a word doesn't look right, hand that student a dictionary to check the spelling.

5. After you have led students through the last line or two of type, tell them to continue on their own through the rest of the story, uncovering one word at a time, working from the bottom to the top of the story, and saying the words aloud as they look at them. Tell them to underline any other words that they think might be misspelled.

6. When students are finished, go through the story aloud, asking individuals to look up words in the dictionary as they tell you they suspect a misspelling. Use the list below to keep track of the errors—mistakes are listed in order of their appearance in the story, with corrections following:

> complement, compliment
>
> affects, effects
>
> florescent, fluorescent
>
> parafin, paraffin
>
> alot, a lot
>
> mispellings, misspellings
>
> worse, worst
>
> excell, excel
>
> sieze, seize
>
> procede, proceed
>
> judgeing, judging
>
> gerbill, gerbil
>
> toothake, toothache
>
> alright, all right
>
> tommorrow, tomorrow
>
> arguements, arguments
>
> principle, principal
>
> wierdest, weirdest

The following story contains many misspelled words. See how many you can find.

"Good morning," said the teacher. "Today I will return your midterm essays. First, I'd like to complement Amy on her essay 'The Affects of Florescent Lights on Parafin Candles.'

"Alot of you didn't do as well as Amy. Joe, your essay was filled with mispellings. It's the worse I've seen in years. If you wish to excell in this class, I suggest you sieze a dictionary before you procede with the next assignment.

"By the way, Vanessa, after judgeing all of the essays, I found yours to be the best in the class. Good job."

Joe raised his hand, and the teacher called on him. "I didn't pass in my essay last week because my gerbill had a toothake. I had to take her to the dentist," said Joe.

"Alright," said the teacher, "but I want your essay tommorrow, and no arguements about it or you will have to see the principle. That's the wierdest excuse I have ever heard."

48

© 1994 by Incentive Publications, Inc., Nashville, TN

Shape It!

To the Teacher:

The word "revision" means, literally, to see again. Sometimes writers are so close to their own work that they fail to "see" what they have written—they see only what they *think* they wrote. Examining and analyzing the writing of others can give students clues to what to look for in revising their own writing. The following activity focuses on the shape or overall organizational structure of a piece of writing. After analyzing organizational structure in published writing, students should be able to see more clearly the organizational pattern of their own writing.

Materials:

Carefully select pieces of writing that illustrate each of the following shape descriptions. Make photocopies.

THE INVERTED PYRAMID:
Reporters use this organizational plan for newswriting. All the important facts are in the first one or two paragraphs. Remaining lesser details are tagged on to the end of the story so that the editor can "cut" the story from the bottom if space on the page is limited.

THE LIST ARTICLE:
Usually found in magazines, this organization is used quite often in how-to-do-it articles. Items in the list may be numbered or preceded by bullets (a typographical device, such as a solid ball or square, used to highlight each item).

THE SPATIAL RELATIONSHIP DESCRIPTION:
This writing structure is useful for presenting the physical location of people or objects—in a room, on a street, on a map. Paragraphs, or sometimes whole stories, may use this organizational plan.

MAIN FEATURE WITH A SIDEBAR TREATMENT:
Magazine and newspaper writers often use "sidebars" or little stories to supplement larger stories on the same topic. For example, a newspaper story on year-round schooling might be accompanied by a smaller sidebar story in which the writer interviews students who give their opinions on year-round schooling.

Other Materials:

- Large white marshmallows
- Small colored marshmallows or gumdrops
- Toothpicks

Time Frame:

- Demonstration—10 minutes
- Each example—30 minutes (building and discussion)

Shape It Activity

1. Demonstration: Explain to students that every good piece of writing must be clearly organized to help the reader understand it. Experienced writers "build" their written works from a clear plan, much as a carpenter or architect works from a blueprint. (If your students have used the satellite outline in Part II of this book, remind them that the satellite helped them plan their essays.) Instruct students to look at a textbook and ask: Who is the writer? How is the book organized to help the reader understand the material?

    Ask students to turn to the Table of Contents page. Explain that most texts are organized into units and chapters. Select a white marshmallow and tell students it represents Unit I. How many chapters are in Unit I? Use the small colored marshmallows to represent chapters. Using a toothpick, attach the correct number of small colored marshmallows to the white one. Build Unit II in the same way and attach it to Unit I. Continue until the Table of Contents is built. Tell students to close their books. From the model you have built, instruct the students to reconstruct the Table of Contents as best they remember. How did the outline structure help the reader?

2. Now it is your students' turn to "build" a writing structure. Arrange students in small groups and distribute photocopies of a story written using the inverted pyramid organizational pattern. Distribute plenty of marshmallows and toothpicks to each group. The members of each group should read the story and discuss the organization plan used by the writer. They should then make a written outline of the writing, and build a toothpick and marshmallow structure that represents the outline.

3. Gather the class and discuss with each group the written outlines and the structures for the inverted pyramid.

4. Repeat steps 2 and 3 for the next photocopied writing sample, as time permits. Later, you might ask students to make structures of their own writing assignments.

PART IV

Writing Projects

The techniques given in the first three parts of this book can be used individually or mixed and matched for use in all three stages of the writing process. For example:

Assignment: story "My Favorite Person"
Prewriting Technique: dialogue journal
Writing Technique: freewrite in the dark
Revision Technique: peer edit, proofread out loud

Assignment: essay "If I Were Principal for a Day"
Prewriting Technique: brainstorm
Writing Technique: reporter's formula
Revision Technique: cut and paste, proofread out loud

Assignment: poem "A Place I Love"
Prewriting Technique: warm-up exercise
Writing Technique: satellite outline
Revision Technique: peer edit, proofread out loud

Assignment: report "History of My Town"
Prewriting Technique: talk it out on tape
Writing Technique: storyboard
Revision Technique: shape it, proofread out loud

Experiment with using different techniques on the writing projects that follow.

Write for Publication

Writers of all ages have to keep their readers in mind. One way to encourage young writers to consider their readers is to have them write for publication. Many magazines and newsletters publish material written by young readers. Just because a magazine is for young people, however, doesn't mean its editors accept student work. Listed below are some publications that do accept student work. For a more complete listing, consult *Market Guide for Young Writers* by Kathy Henderson and *Children's Writer's and Illustrator's Market*, Lisa Carpenter, editor.

Boys' Life, 1325 Walnut Hill Ln., Box 152079, Irving, TX 75015

Children's Playmate and Children's Digest, Box 567, Indianapolis, IN 46206

Highlights for Children, 803 Church St., Honesdale, PA 18431

The McGuffey Writer, 5128 Westgate Dr., Oxford, OH 45056

National Geographic World, 17th and M St., Washington, DC 20036

Stone Soup, Children's Art Foundation, Box 83, Santa Cruz, CA 95063

Writing (grades 7-12), 60 Revere Dr., Northbrook, IL 60062

Step by step, here's how to guide your students toward publishing their writing:

1. Obtain sample copies of magazines that publish children's work. If you cannot obtain copies in the library or at the newsstand, write to the editors to inquire whether sample copies are available and if there is a cost.

2. Allow students time to study the sample copies so they can see the types of writing the editors publish.

3. In class, draft letters to the editors of the magazines to request writer's guidelines. These documents are usually free, but you should send a self-addressed, stamped envelope along with your request.

4. Allow students to study the writer's guidelines, which are the editor's suggestions for what to write and how to prepare work for publication.

Now your students are ready to write.

Write To Win

You can plan and organize a classroom competition to reward excellent writing. Have students vote for their favorite pieces of writing in different categories. Also, many companies, associations, and publishers sponsor writer's contests. Listed below are a few of these. Note: Rules may change annually. Be sure to request current contest information, deadlines, entry fees, and age requirements.

Byline **Magazine Student Page Contest**, P.O. Box 130596, Edmond, OK 73140

Cricket League, *Cricket* **Magazine**, 315 5th St., Peru, IL 61354

Hoot Awards, Writing Contest, *Owl* **Magazine**, 56 The Esplanade, Toronto, ON M4V 1G2, Canada

The National Written and Illustrated By . . . Awards Contest for Students, Landmark Editions, Inc., Box 4469, Kansas City, MO 64127

Publish-A-Book-Contest, Raintree Publishers, 310 W. Wisconsin Ave., Milwaukee, WI 53203

Scholastic Writing Awards, Scholastic, Inc., 730 Broadway, New York, NY 10003

We Are Writers, Too! Creative With Words Publications, Box 223226, Carmel, CA 93922

Young Writers' Contest, Young Writers' Contest Foundation, Box 6092, McLean, VA 22106

For a more complete listing of contests and awards for writers, see Kathy Henderson's *Market Guide for Young Writers* or the current *Writer's Market* (Writer's Digest Books).

A Writing Adventure

Students take field trips to learn about science, nature, and history. Why not plan a field trip to learn about writing? Students don't have to travel far from the classroom to get a new perspective on their writing topics. For example, allow students to rough-draft their essays on sports as they sit in the gym or outside on the bleachers. Or you might introduce a report assignment about animals during a trip to the zoo. A change of place might bring a change of pace!

Younger students may need a set of probe questions to take along with them on their writing adventure.

For example:

1. What did I see?
2. What did I hear?
3. What did I taste?
4. What did I smell?
5. What did I feel?

Another idea is to send students on a writing adventure and then have them "report" their experiences newspaper style. Different students could be sent to cover different "beats": the office, the cafeteria, the gym, the rest room, the teachers' lounge, etc.

A Writer's Escape

If you can't take a writing adventure beyond the classroom, bring a bit of excitement into the classroom. Here are a few suggestions for creating a lively environment in which your students will want to write.

- Provide music during writing times. Try to match the music to the spirit of the writing assignment—upbeat, lively music during creative prewriting exercises; mellow background music for revision times.

- Vary writing times. Some students are able to complete whole drafts in a single sitting, while others may prefer to work in smaller segments of time. Some students may produce their most creative ideas in the morning, while others work better after lunch. Be flexible when you schedule in-class writing assignments.

- Create a writer's refuge in your classroom—a place where individuals can "hole up" for a few minutes and work on a piece of writing. The refuge could be a desk behind a folding screen, a piece of carpet on the floor, or a folding cot for students who like to write while lying down. Remove the door from a storage cupboard, line the cupboard with an old rug, and let your student writer crawl inside to write. Remove the staples from a refrigerator or stove carton to create a "writing box."

- Provide a variety of writing supplies. It can be fun to write with a fountain pen or a calligraphy pen instead of a pencil; on unlined paper instead of lined; with fluorescent ink instead of black; with white ink on black construction paper. Other writer's tools include a dictionary and thesaurus (the computerized versions are fun if you can afford them), writer's books and magazines (see pages 78 and 79 of this book), scissors and glue sticks for revisions, and stamps and envelopes for writing letters.

Launch a Campaign

Campaigns—political or advertising—offer a wealth of opportunity for writing. For example, one class developed an advertising campaign for the school's annual Valentine's Day dance. The campaign produced student writing in the following formats:

- Poster copy to advertise the school Valentine's Day dance
- Print advertisement placed in the parents' newsletter
- Valentine's Day verses printed in the dance program
- Written announcement to be read over the school's public address system
- Written invitations to family and friends to attend the dance
- News story for the community paper

Many school events and issues are opportunities for campaign writing. Here are a few suggestions:

- Anti-litter or promotion of recycling
- Read a good book
- Teacher/staff appreciation day
- School concerts

Share It

Encourage your students to share their writing with readers outside the classroom. A popular way to do this is to make a "book" which requires typing and duplicating student work. Parents are sometimes willing to help out with the typing; however, don't let the lack of a typist stop you from publishing your students' work. Other forms of "publication" include:

- Audio tapes of students reading their work, perhaps with sound effects

- Video tapes of students reading their work, using student "actors" to dramatize when appropriate

- Posters or displays combining artwork with a written piece

- Live readers' theatre in which students read their work to invited listeners

Correspond with an Author

Some of the best advice for young writers comes from professional writers—people who use words to make a living. Organize a class letter to request specific writing advice from the author of a favorite book. Check with the school librarian for a list of most-read-and-loved books checked out by your students. Brainstorm with the class to make a list of questions to ask the author. Send the letter to the author in care of the publishing company named in his or her books. Include a self-addressed, stamped envelope to facilitate the response.

Listed below are some recent Caldecott and Newbery Medal winners:

Newbery Winners

1988 **Lincoln: A PhotoBiography**
Russe Freedman
Clarion Books
Houghton Mifflin Co.
215 Park Ave. S.
New York, NY 10003

1989 **Joyful Noise**
Paul Fleischman
Harper and Row
Harpercollins Books
10 E. 53rd St.
New York, NY 10022

1990 **Number the Stars**
Lois Lowry
Houghton Mifflin Co.
Children's Trade Books
2 Park St.
Boston, MA 02108

1991 **Maniac Magee**
Jerry Spinelli
34 Beacon St.
Boston, MA 02108

1992 **Shiloh**
Phyllis Naylor
Atheneum Publishers
Macmillan Children's Book Group
866 Third Ave.
New York, NY 10022

1993 **Missing May**
Cynthia Rylant
Orchard/Richard Jackson
95 Madison Ave.
New York, NY 10016

1994 **The Giver**
Lois Lowry
Houghton Mifflin Co.
Children's Trade Books
2 Park Street
Boston, MA 02108

Caldecott Winners

1988 **Owl Moon**
Jane Yolen
Philomel Books
200 Madison Ave.
New York, NY 10016

1989 **Song and Dance Man**
Karen Ackerman
Knopf Books for Young Readers
Random House, Inc.
8th floor, 225 Park Ave. S.
New York, NY 10003

1990 **Lon Po Po**
Ed Young
Philomel Books
200 Madison Ave.
New York, NY 10016

1991 **Black and White**
David Macaulay
Houghton Mifflin Co.
Children's Trade Books
2 Park St.
Boston, MA 02108

1992 **Tuesday**
David Weisner
Clarion Books
Houghton Mifflin Co.
215 Park Ave. S.
New York, NY 10003

1993 **Mirette on the High Wire**
Emily Arnold McCully
Putnam
200 Madison Ave.
New York, NY 10016

1994 **Grandfather's Journey**
Allen Say
Houghton Mifflin Co.
Children's Trade Books
2 Park St.
Boston, MA 02108

Note: The Newbery Medal is awarded annually by the American Library Association to the author of the most distinguished contribution to children's literature. The Caldecott Medal is awarded annually to the illustrator of the most distinguished American picture book. Author and illustrator may differ.

Walking Compositions

This idea is a variation of the Writing Adventure project described on page 56 of this book. The Walking Composition activity is described in Tom Liner and Dan Kirby's book, *Inside Out, Developmental Strategies for Teaching Writing* (Boynton Cook Publishers, Inc.). Their book is a rich resource for teachers of writing. Here's how to send your students on a walking composition.

1. Instruct students to take a pencil and notebook; set a time limit for a walking tour of the school building, grounds, campus, or whatever limits you set. You may wish to divide the students into small groups and send them off with specific maps or itineraries.

2. Tell students to be "sensory sponges," to soak up and write down as many sensory experiences as they can. They are to be careful observers as they walk, recording their experiences much as a CIA agent might. Instruct students to talk as little as possible as they walk.

3. Follow up the walking tour with an in-class discussion of the students' observations and notes. Then give them a writing assignment in which they may use their notes.

A Picture's Worth in Words

How many different ideas can one picture inspire? As the saying goes, is a picture really worth a thousand words? To find out, guide your students in this simple experiment. Find a picture in a magazine or in the library's poster collection and display it so every student can see it. (Suggestion: You might find something interesting or funny in your own photo collection. Have the print made into a slide and project it onto the wall.)

Without any discussion, ask your students to freewrite about what they see, but tell them that the piece of writing will not be graded. This is simply a warm-up exercise. After 10 minutes, discuss the students' observations and compose a list on the board. How many different things did the students observe? What characteristics did they observe in common? What unusual observations were made? You can compose their ideas in a list, as a satellite outline, or as a storyboard. Be sure to get every idea up on the board where students can see them. Are there a thousand words? Probably not, but there will certainly be plenty of different topics on which to write.

Instruct students to choose one of the ideas on the board as a topic for a short essay. This activity is excellent practice for students who have difficulty "narrowing" their essay topics.

Family Tree

The family tree idea is suggested in the book *Writing To Grow* by Mary Louise Holly (Heinemann Educational Books, Inc.). As a writing activity, the family tree helps students to organize writing from a chart and to define relationships. It also provides a basis for autobiographical and biographical writing.

Begin by constructing your own family tree. Go back as many generations as practical, filling in names and birth, death, and marriage dates if known. Post the diagram for students to see. Begin the discussion with yourself, telling students when and where you were born and any other particulars of your life. Then move on to your parents and grandparents.

Ask students to construct their own family trees, giving them plenty of time to have their family members fill in the gaps. You may wish to use the reproducible on page 66. When the family trees are finished, use them as a basis for in-class writing assignments. Here are some topic ideas:

1. **Autobiographical Writing:**
   Write about your life, the day you were born (or adopted), your life today, your future.

2. **Biographical Writing:**
   Write about a member of your family (mother, sister, father, brother, etc.), how your relative (pick one) has influenced your life, what your grandparents remember about their childhood.

3. Chronological Writing:

Using the family tree chart, write about the development of your family, beginning with your ancestors at the very top of the tree.

4. Descriptive Writing:

Describe your experiences in filling in the family tree chart. How much did you know already? Who helped fill in the gaps? What did you learn that you hadn't known before you started the project?

5. Creative Writing:

Using the family tree as inspiration, write a poem or short story based on biographical or autobiographical information.

(Note: You can find many useful tips for writing about the results of family tree research in the booklet, *Family Folklore: How To Record Family Stories and Traditions for Genealogical Research.* To get the guide, send $1 to Consumer Information Center–P, P.O. Box 100, Pueblo, CO 81002.)

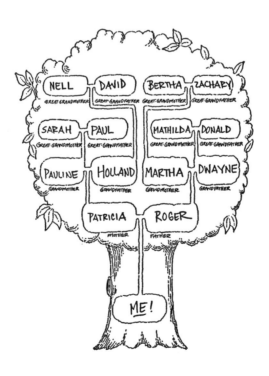

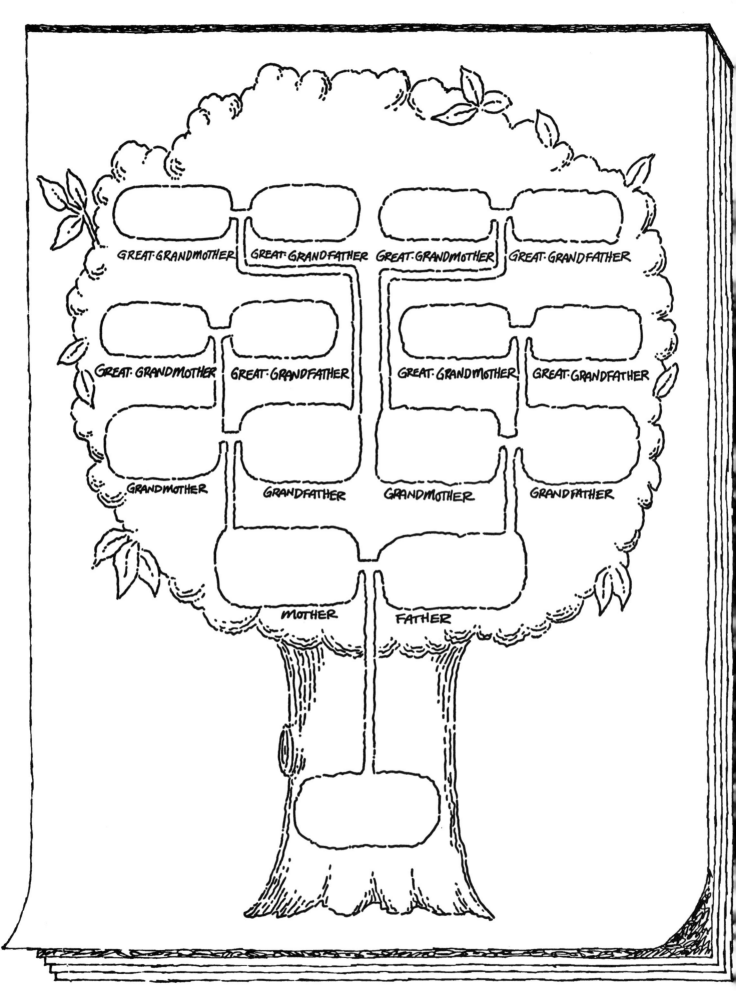

GREAT·GRANDMOTHER GREAT·GRANDFATHER GREAT·GRANDMOTHER GREAT·GRANDFATHER

GREAT·GRANDMOTHER GREAT·GRANDFATHER GREAT·GRANDMOTHER GREAT·GRANDFATHER

GRANDMOTHER GRANDFATHER GRANDMOTHER GRANDFATHER

MOTHER FATHER

Picture Poems

For very young students and for those frustrated with writing because of past failures, picture poetry writing is an activity that practically guarantees instant success. A picture poem consists of words or letters arranged on a blank page to suggest an image—a verbal picture. Verbal poets aren't concerned with punctuation or sentence structure. In fact, most students will think of this project as an art activity rather than a writing assignment.

On the following page are some picture poems created by fourth grader Katy Seguin. Your students can write picture poems suggested by the following words—or let them come up with their own ideas.

Concrete Images	Abstract Images
hot dog	happy
egg	sad
sun	music
moon	thirsty
waves	pain
footprint	sleepy
rabbit	peace
clock	hot/cold
pizza	fear
flower	comfortable

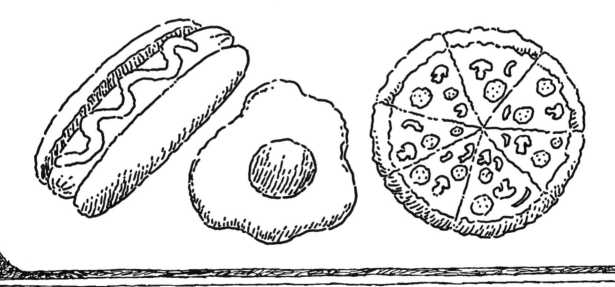

Sun (radiating text):
I really love the sun. ☆★The sun shines down on the earth and makes it so everyone ... The sun is warm. I think the sun is a great thing to think ... is not hot and yellow. ... so hot, don't you think? root

Flower:
flower middle • Flowers are beautiful. Bees love flowers a lot. I love flowers. smell good. There are millions of them. They are all different. This is the stem. It is green. They make nice bouquets.

Leaf:
★This is the leaf. It's attached to the stem.

Apple:
Stem · Leaf leaf · Skin Skin Skin Skin Mantle Mantle Mantle Mantle Mantle Mantle Mantle Core Core Core Core Seeds Core Mantle Mantle Mantle Skin Skin Skin Skin Skin Skin Skin Mantle Mantle Mantle

Katy Seguin

Words of Wisdom

Advice—no one gets more instruction from well-meaning friends and relatives than youngsters. Youngsters get advice from parents, from teachers, from older (and sometimes younger) siblings, and others. The advice may range from the classic (never speak to strangers) to the unusual (eat carrots to improve your eyesight).

Several authors have collected and sorted bits of advice and published them as little books of reminders on how to live successfully. H. Jackson Brown, Jr.'s books of advice have made the best seller lists and have been turned into posters, calendars, and greeting cards. Talks are under way for a TV show based on the books' advice. You and your students can use these books as models for discussion. Then collect advice from your own friends and families and "publish" your own book.

A few recent advice-giving books are:

Writers on Writing by Jon Winokur (Running Press). This volume contains a section of advice from professional writers to young writers.

Live and Learn and Pass It On and *Life's Little Instruction Book*. Both of these books are written and compiled by H. Jackson Brown, Jr. (Rutledge Hill Press).

Here's how to get started on your own collection of folk wisdom:

1. Brainstorm sources of advice. Your class list might include the following:

    - parents

    - grandparents

    - siblings

    - teachers

    - principal

    - custodian

    - cafeteria workers

    - office staff

2. Reproduce the advice questionnaire on page 71 and give one to each student. Ask students to write about the advice they have been given on the five response topics. Give them a week to think about and complete the assignment.

3. Collect and discuss the responses as a class.

4. Assign a group of students to cut apart the responses on the dotted lines, sorting the pieces into five piles which represent each advice category. Eliminate any duplicates.

5. Share the collection! If you are lucky enough to have a typist, publish the collection in print form. If not, arrange labels on a bulletin board to represent each response category, and post as many responses as will fit underneath each label. Or you may tape record or videotape student readings of the advice.

Advice Questionnaire

Name _____

The best advice I ever got about eating came from _____
She/He said:

- -

Name _____

The best advice I ever got about dressing/grooming came from _____
He/She said:

- -

Name _____

The best advice I ever got about behaving came from_____
She/He said:

- -

Name _____

The best advice I ever got about going to school came from _____
He/She said:

- -

Name _____

The best advice I ever got about _____ came from _____
She/He said:

- -

Time in a Bottle

Filling a time capsule can be an exciting project for your students, and writing a "Book of Record" is a follow-up assignment students will find fun. Step by step, here's how to approach the challenge.

1. Share the information about the first time capsule with your students. (Read aloud or reproduce page 73.)

2. Choose a container and storage spot for a class or school time capsule. Determine an opening date for the capsule.

3. Use the five categories set up by the engineers of the first time capsule to determine what mementos you want to leave to the future. Collect these items and display them on a table.

4. Individually or as a class write a "Book of Record" for the time capsule.

5. Deposit the mementos in the time capsule and bury or store it for the future. Distribute the "Book of Record" in several places around the school—in the library, in the office, with other teachers, etc.

Time in a Bottle

Fifty feet beneath the ground on the site of the 1939 New York World's Fair, the world's first time capsule was buried. After months of discussions, the engineers who buried the capsule decided that the contents of the time capsule should include five different categories of items:

1. Articles of common use—eyeglasses, camera, light bulb, etc.

2. Textiles and materials—cloth, rocks, plastics, etc.

3. Miscellaneous items—seeds, money, etc.

4. "Essay of our Times"—a microfilm including maps, history, the Bible, a dictionary, etc.

5. Motion pictures—newsreels, historic events, etc. Instructions on how to build a movie projector and microfilm viewer were also included.

The time capsule will stay buried for 5,000 years, until the year 6939 A.D. The challenge to the engineers who buried it was how to leave word to future historians as to the location of the time capsule. It is possible that the location could be covered by water or ice in the year 6939! For this reason, the engineers wrote the "Book of Record," which describes the capsule, its location and its contents. It also contains a key to the English language. Three thousand copies of the "Book of Record" are now in libraries around the world.

Writer's Showcase

Reward your students by making their writing the center of attention. Display student writing in the classroom, but don't stop there. Here's a list of additional places to display student work:

- Hallways
- School library
- School office
- Offices of the Board of Education
- Cafeteria
- Public library of your town
- Town hall
- Fine arts museum
- Other schools
- Education department or writing center of a local university
- Store windows
- Hospital lobbies
- Nursing home lounges

To make your writing showcase interesting:

- Frame or mount student work before posting.
- "Antique" student work by tearing or burning the edges and streaking the paper with a wet tea bag.
- Display writing with pictures or illustrations.
- Include your own writing in the showcase.
- Take pictures of your students as they write; display these with their works.
- Include unfinished works in the showcase, including drafts and works-in-progress.
- Incorporate the ceiling and the floor into your writer's showcase; enlarge poetry and hang it from the ceiling; laminate it and attach it to the floor.
- Change the showcase often to give all students a chance to see their writing on display. Don't insist, however, that a student display his or her writing if the student is reluctant.

Pen Names

In her excellent book *If You're Trying To Teach Kids How To Write, You've Gotta Have This Book!* (Incentive Publications), author Marjorie Frank suggests that writing under a pseudonym can be a real tension-dissolver for kids. There are a couple of reasons for this. First, creating a pen name allows the writer to become someone else—someone who is not afraid to write. Second, a pen name offers the writer anonymity. Students may be more willing to write and share freely under the cover of a pen name.

To help your students think up creative and meaningful pen names, share the background information on pages 76 and 77 about the lives and pen names of some professional authors.

How Writers Choose Their Pen Names

Writers like to play with words. Since a name consists of words, it should not be surprising that writers often play with their names to create pen names or pseudonyms. Some writers create pen names that reflect an important person or event in their lives. For example:

George Eliot is the pen name of novelist Mary Ann Evans. She chose the name "George" to honor the love of her life, George Henry Lewes. "Eliot" is actually a rough anagram (letter scramble), meaning "to L(ewes) I Owe iT." Therefore, the pen name of George Eliot came to be a tribute to the one she loved.

When Edward Stratemeyer first began to write, he asked his mom for advice about a pseudonym. She suggested Arthur (because it sounds like "author") Winfield (because she thought he could win in the field of writing). Thus, the Rover Boys stories were written under the pen name of Arthur M. Winfield.

Mark Twain is the pen name of Samuel Langhorne Clemens, author of *The Adventures of Tom Sawyer* and *The Adventures of Huckleberry Finn.* When he was a boy, Clemens longed to be a riverboat pilot on the Mississippi River. After training, he finally received his license. Although he later left the river for a writing career, his love for the river was reflected in his pen name—"mark twain" is a riverman's call for safe water, signaling the depth of the river.

It is not unusual for the same writer to have several pen names, depending on what he or she is writing. Here are three techniques often used by writers when they are creating pen names:

- **Puns:**
  A pun is a play on words. Some names are easy to pun. For example, John Rhode is the pen name for writer Cecil John Street. Michael East is the pen name for Morris West.

- **Anagrams:**
  Anagrams mix up letters of words to create new words. For example, Melusa Moolson is the pen name of Samuel Solomon. John Langdon writes under the pen name of John Gannold.

- **Tandem:**
  When two or more authors work together (collaborate) on a piece of writing, they may write under one name formed by combination. For example, the pen name Kelly Ross is actually a combination of the names of writers Audrey Kelley and William Ross.

Your assignment: Create one or several pen names for yourself.

Writer's Resources

If you have a writing center or a library in your classroom, you'll want to include a few of the following books and magazines written just for writers about their craft. Although the following resources are aimed at writers, not teachers of writing, you'll find these publications rich resources for writing project ideas.

Books for Young Writers

A Beginner's Guide To Getting Published edited by Kirk Polking (Writer's Digest Books). A how-to- and where-to-publish guide for new and young writers. 1987.

Children's Writer's and Illustrator's Market (Writer's Digest Books). An annual listing of places to sell writing and illustrations. Includes a section listing markets for young writers and illustrators. Updated annually.

How I Came To Be a Writer by Phyllis Naylor (Atheneum). Author tells readers about writing as a career. 1978.

Market Guide for Young Writers by Kathy Henderson (Shoe Tree Press). How to prepare writing for publication, with a listing of publishers. 1990.

What's Your Story? A Young Person's Guide To Writing Fiction by Marion Dane Bauer (Clarion Books). A how-to guide for aspiring young writers. 1992.

Where Do You Get Your Ideas? by Sandy Asher (Walker). Author tells readers where writing ideas come from and how they can generate their own ideas. 1987.

Write Your Own Story by Vivian Dubrovin (Franklin Watts). Guide to writing about personal experiences. 1984.

Writing Books for Young People by James Cross Giblin (The Writer, Inc.). Covers all aspects of juvenile book writing. 1990.

Writer's Resources, cont.

Magazines for Young Writers

Merlyn's Pen: The National Magazines of Student Writing, P.O. Box 1058, Dept. WR, East Greenwich, RI 02818.

Teacher's and Writer's Magazine, Teacher's and Writer's Collaborative, 5 Union Square West, New York, NY 10003.

Writer's Digest, Subscription Department, Box 2123, Harlan, IA 51593 (toll free 800-333-0133).